help me UNDERSTAND™

Feeling **Embarrassment**
& Learning **Humor**™

REAL mvpkids®

Gabby Bears with Embarrassment

SOPHIA DAY®

Written by Megan Johnson *Illustrated by* Stephanie Strouse

The Sophia Day® Creative Team-

Stephanie Strouse, Megan Johnson,

Kayla Pearson, Timothy Zowada, Carol Sauder, Mel Sauder

A **special thank you** to our team of reviewers who graciously give us feedback, edits and help ensure that our products remain accurate, applicable and genuinely diverse.

Published and Distributed by MVP Kids Media, LLC -
Mesa, Arizona, USA
Printed by Prosperous Printing Inc. -
Shenzhen, China

Designed by Stephanie Strouse

DOM June 2019, Job # 02-008-01

May your childhood be filled with adventure, your days with hope and your learnings with wisdom, and may you continuously grow as an MVP Kid, preparing to lead a responsible, meaningful life.

–SOPHIA DAY

"I'm so excited, Oso*!"

Gabby said to her teddy bear. "My first overnight camp! I have all the clothes I need. What else should I pack?"

*__Oso__ is Spanish for "bear."

Gabby searched for things she would miss while she was gone. She put a favorite book, her diary and some colored pens into her backpack.

Hesitating at her family photo, she realized how much she was going to miss everyone. Would other kids tease her if she brought the picture?

I'll keep it in my bag.
No one will see it,
she thought.

She wrapped the picture frame in her blanket to keep it safe. Finally, she tucked in her teddy bear.

"You can come, Oso, but you'll have to get used to being zipped inside my bag. I don't think kids take stuffed animals to camp."

“Ready to go?” her mom asked.
“Mrs. Patel will be here any minute to pick you up.”

“All ready!” said Gabby.

Gabby set her bags on the porch and waited by the stables until her ride came.

Abuela* was helping her younger sister, Verónica, mount a horse.

*__Abuela__ is Spanish for "Grandmother."

When Verónica noticed Gabby,
she waved, lost focus and fell.

Verónica wasn't hurt, but
she was embarrassed.

Gabby listened as Abuela recited what she always tells kids when they fall:

"It's okay to feel embarrassed.
Everyone does sometimes.
Pick yourself up and laugh it off.
Let the world know you're fine."

Everyone heard the car coming up the gravel road. The whole family stopped what they were doing to say goodbye to Gabby.

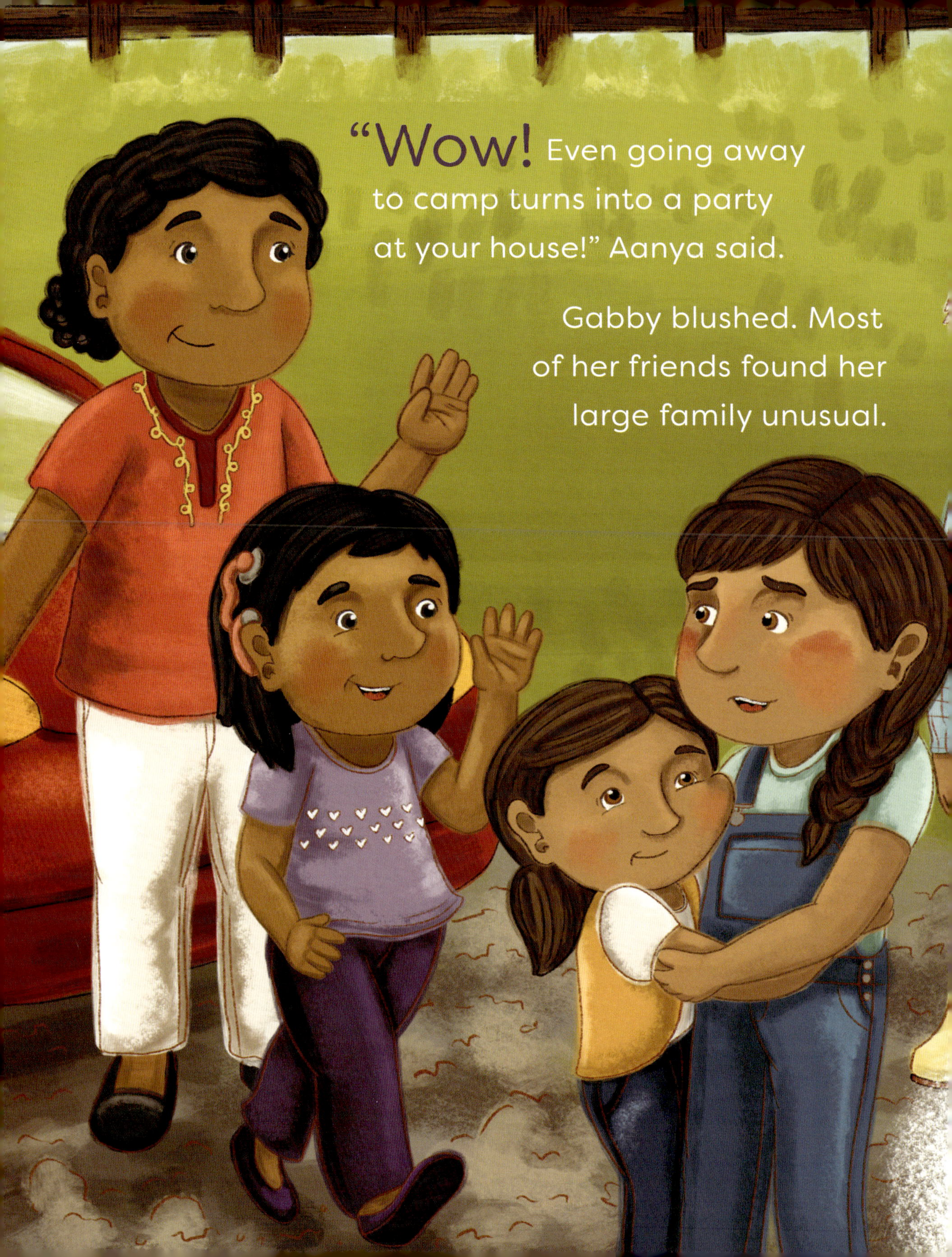

"Wow! Even going away to camp turns into a party at your house!" Aanya said.

Gabby blushed. Most of her friends found her large family unusual.

She repeated
Abuela's saying in her mind.

It's okay to feel embarrassed.
Everyone does sometimes.
Pick yourself up and laugh it off.
Let the world know you're fine.

“There’s never a dull moment,”

Gabby said with a smile. She hugged Verónica, then peeled her sister’s arms off her waist.

Gabby's dad bent down to get her bags. She quickly took her backpack from him. "I'll hold on to this one!"

After giving hugs to her family, Gabby climbed in next to Aanya.

When they arrived at camp, the girls ran to the swings while Mrs. Patel went to check them in.

Gabby looked around
at all the kids.

She hoped
she would fit in
with them.

"Let's go find our bunks," Aanya said.

"Okay!" Gabby pumped her legs one last time, then launched herself off the swing. Oh no! Her zipper pull was stuck on the chain!

With a sudden jerk, her backpack slipped off her shoulders, and Gabby landed flat on her back.

Catching her breath, Gabby looked around and saw all of her private things scattered around the playground.

She was so embarrassed!

Aanya reached out a hand to help her up. "Are you okay, Gabby?"

"Yes. Quick! Help me get my stuff!" Gabby cried.

A boy handed Oso to her. "Your bear hit me when your stuff went flying. Here you go, *Bear Girl.*"

"Sorry!" Gabby quickly grabbed Oso. The whole world had seen what happened, and now she would be known as "Bear Girl" all week!

"Let me help you," the boy said.

"No, I've got it."

The girls gathered her things as quickly as they could and ran to the cabin.

Stephanie was here
Kayla and MEGAN BFFs
John 3:16

"I want to go home!" Gabby cried.

"It wasn't that bad," Aanya said.

"But everyone saw my blanket, my picture and my teddy bear. I'm so embarrassed."

"It'll be okay," Aanya reassured her friend. "I know it feels like everyone was watching, but it was just a few kids. It feels much worse than it was."

“You really think so?”

“I’m sure of it. Trust me. I have a lot of experience with people staring at me.” Aanya pointed to her cochlear implants.

Gabby had been friends with her for so long that she didn't see them as unusual at all, but she remembered being curious when the girls first met.

“What do you do about it?” asked Gabby.

“Sometimes I make a joke to show people that I'm comfortable with myself. I act confident even when I don't feel it,” Aanya said.

“That’s right. Abuela says no one can laugh at you as long as you’re laughing, too.”

Gabby picked up her bear.

“¡Qué Oso!”* she said, laughing.

“It’s okay to feel embarrassed.
Everyone does sometimes.
Pick yourself up and laugh it off.
Let the world know you’re fine.”

****“¡Qué oso!”*** is a Spanish expression that means “How embarrassing!”

Gabby knew that hiding away in the cabin would only make things worse. She'd feel confident as long as she stuck with her friend.

"An embarrassment is only as big of a deal as you let it be. Let's go face the world again, Bear Girl!" Aanya said.

Gabby laughed at her new nickname. Maybe the boy hadn't meant it to be rude. She imagined what it must have been like for him to be hit with her flying teddy bear. It was sort of funny, after all.

"Come on, I'll show you the lake!" Aanya said. Gabby and Aanya went exploring and met some of the other campers. No one mentioned her embarrassing moment.

Maybe the whole world didn't see, or if they did, they don't really care, she thought.

That night, as Gabby was getting ready for bed, she pulled her bear out of her backpack. "What a day it's been, Oso," she mumbled. She was so glad she had decided to bring him.

"Psst. Hey!" The girl in the next bunk whispered to get her attention. "I'm glad you brought your bear. I was afraid I'd be the only one." She showed Gabby her stuffed unicorn, while the other girls brought their animals out, too.

Gabby realized that what she thought was embarrassing was actually really common.

In fact, most embarrassing moments are common mishaps, like falling down, forgetting something or showing the whole world your teddy bear. It helps to know you're **not the only one** who experiences embarrassment.

Not everyone was as kind as the girls in her cabin. Some kids teased her, but Gabby learned to stick with friends who showed true kindness. Even Liam, the boy who first called her "Bear Girl" became a good friend.

On their last night together, everyone gathered around campfires to make s'mores.

Liam reached for a marshmallow and fell backward off the log. Aanya held her breath. She almost laughed, but **she didn't want to hurt Liam's feelings.** It can be hard to control laughter when something surprising happens.

Even Gabby, who knew a bit about embarrassing falls, had a hard time holding back a giggle.

Gabby reached to help him.

"Are you hurt?" she whispered.

"No. I'm okay," Liam said.

Through the firelight, Gabby could see him blushing.

She told him,

"It's okay to feel embarrassed.
Everyone does sometimes.
Pick yourself up and laugh it off.
Let the world know you're fine."

She smiled widely and added, "Bear Boy."

She pointed at his shadow. The leaves and sticks that were stuck in his hair and the gooey marshmallows on his hand made his shadow look like a bear's. Liam laughed, then Gabby did, too.

He faced the group and gave out a big

"Grrrrrowl!"

Since Liam found humor first, his friends were free to laugh with him.

Growing up can be full of embarrassing moments. Gabby was thankful for friends who could laugh through them **together.**

Blushing hot, embarrassed,
You look around and wonder,
"Did everybody see me
Making such a blunder?"

A dizzy fog surrounds you,
And the whole world clearly sees
All your fears and failures
Tumble open in the breeze.

You quickly try to turn your face
To run and hide away,
Afraid this one mistake defines you
Now through every day.

But it's okay to feel embarrassed.
Everyone does sometimes.
Pick yourself up and laugh it off.
Let the world know you're fine.

If you'll find a bit of humor,
Make a lesser deal of it,
The sooner that you show you're calm,
The sooner they'll forget.

Embarrassments will surely come,
But you know your friends are true
Who check to see that you're okay,
Then laugh *with* - not *at* - you.

LEARN & DISCUSS

Gabby is learning to understand and find humor in times of embarrassment. Learn with Gabby and discuss how you can recover from embarrassing moments, too.

I was excited and nervous about my first camp retreat. I wanted to pack all my most special things, but I wasn't sure what other kids would think about my family photo, my teddy bear and my blanket.

What things would you pack for a week at camp?

Are you unsure what others might think about any of those things?

My abuela always says, "It's okay to feel embarrassed. Everyone does sometimes. Pick yourself up and laugh it off. Let the world know you're fine."

What does it mean to "laugh it off?"

Is it easy or difficult for you to laugh when something embarrassing happens to you?

I first felt embarrassed when Aanya commented on my big family. Families come in all sizes and styles, but it's normal for kids to sometimes be embarrassed about family.

Are you sometimes embarrassed about your family? Why?

What makes your family special?

When my personal things flew all over the playground and my bear hit Liam, he called me "Bear Girl." I felt so embarrassed. I thought that he was making fun of me. He just wanted to be helpful and make friends with me. Sometimes we think people are being mean when that isn't always the case.

Is there a time when you have been embarrassed in front of your peers? Did you think kids were making fun of you? Is it possible they were just trying to help?

Aanya talked with me about how she feels when others stare at her. Her solution is to act confident and make a joke so that others know she is at ease with herself. When you are laughing, others can't really laugh at you. Instead, they're laughing with you.

How would you comfort a friend who feels embarrassed?

What advice would you give to Gabby if you were her friend?

Sometimes when I am embarrassed, I just want to hide. Abuela's saying to "let the world know you're fine" helped me be brave enough to go outside and explore at camp. I'm glad I didn't miss out on the fun!

Have you ever been so embarrassed that you hid and missed out on something?

Have you ever been afraid to try something new because you might be embarrassed?

When Liam fell off the log at the campfire, everyone had a hard time controlling their laughter. Sometimes people laugh when something is sudden or surprising, but they don't intend to be mean.

How did Liam respond? Which friends do you trust to laugh with you through life's embarrassing moments?

How can you help your child overcome embarrassment?

Learning to handle an embarrassing situation is part of becoming resilient and an important factor for success. We all know that embarrassing moments don't end once a person reaches adulthood. Developing a sense of humor and self-compassion will help your child navigate life's many embarrassing moments.

Set an example. Your child is always watching your reactions. When you spill coffee down your shirt, drop a carton of eggs in the grocery store or spit when you talk, don't overreact. Phrases like "I can't believe I did that!" or "How $t^p!d of me!*" tell your child indirectly that mishaps and mistakes are a reason to be ashamed. Handle situations calmly to send a message to your child that these things are not a big deal.

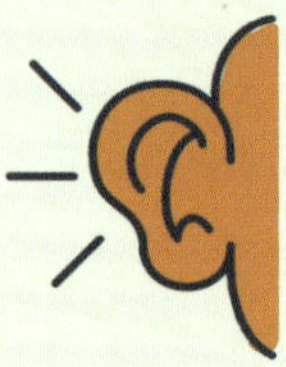

Take it seriously. If your child is expressing embarrassment, listen in a way that shows you take your child's feelings seriously. Downplaying an experience that feels like a very big deal may cause children to feel as if you do not understand or cannot be trusted with their true feelings. At the same time, do not overreact by becoming upset on your child's behalf, which can add to embarrassment.

*$t^p!d is not a typographical error. We just couldn't **bear** to print that word in a children's book!*

Provide empathy and perspective. After listening attentively, consider sharing a similar embarrassing moment you have had. Discuss things that embarrassed you at your child's age. Help children see that embarrassing moments pass and don't dramatically change their life. Provide perspective by asking questions that show where they may be exaggerating the story. Children will often use words such as "everyone" and "always" that are not true. It's likely that not *everyone* saw their mishap, or they aren't always clumsy. Help children step outside of the situation by asking questions about times they have seen other kids fall or drop their lunch tray or other embarrassing situations. Remind them that other kids will easily forget what happened and life will quickly return to normal.

Know when to seek help. The following concerns may develop out of embarrassing situations and may be cause for greater action.

Bullying – If your child is repeatedly made fun of for the same issue or by the same people, it may be a bullying situation. Teachers, school administration or others may need to become involved.

Obsessing – Most embarrassing moments become less important to your child over time. However if your child's reaction seems out of proportion to the situation, results in lost sleep, loss of appetite or excessive worrying, consider talking to your child's pediatrician.

Social Anxiety – Embarrassment can escalate into fear of being embarrassed, causing your child to become avoidant and isolated. If your child begins to panic at the thought of doing everyday activities or going to routine places for fear of embarrassment, they may be experiencing social anxiety. If your child demonstrates excessive social anxiety, therapy can be very effective in helping children return to routine life.

For additional tips and reference information, visit ***www.mvpkids.com****.*

Meet the

mvpkids®

featured in

Gabby Bears with Embarrassment™

GABBY GONZÁLEZ

AANYA PATEL

LIAM JOHNSON

Also featuring...

MIGUEL GONZÁLEZ
Grandfather
"Abuelo"

ROSA MARIA GONZÁLEZ
Grandmother
"Abuela"

JOSEFINA PÉREZ
Grandmother
"Tata"

MR. FERNANDO GONZÁLEZ
"Papa"

MRS. MARIA CAMILLA GONZÁLEZ
"Mama"

JOSÉ GONZÁLEZ
Brother

PEDRO GONZÁLEZ
Brother

VERÓNICA GONZÁLEZ
Sister

CARLOS GONZÁLEZ
Brother

help me UNDERSTAND™

Elementary

Ages 6-12

Help your children grow in understanding emotions by collecting the entire **Help Me Understand™** series!

*Our **Help Me Understand™** series for elementary readers shares the stories of our MVP Kids® learning to understand and manage specific emotions. Readers will gain tools to take responsibility for their own emotions and develop healthy relationships.*

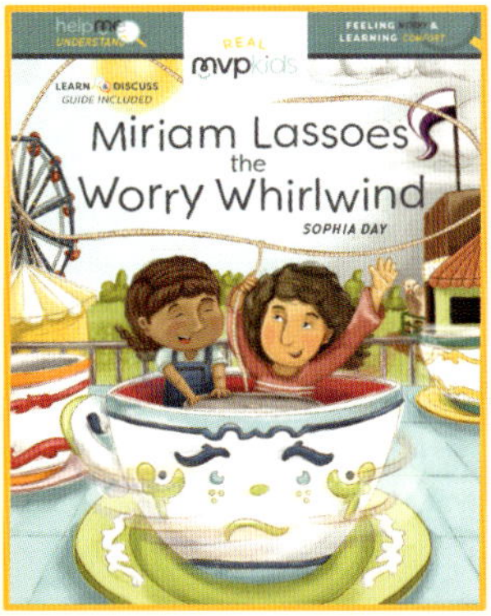

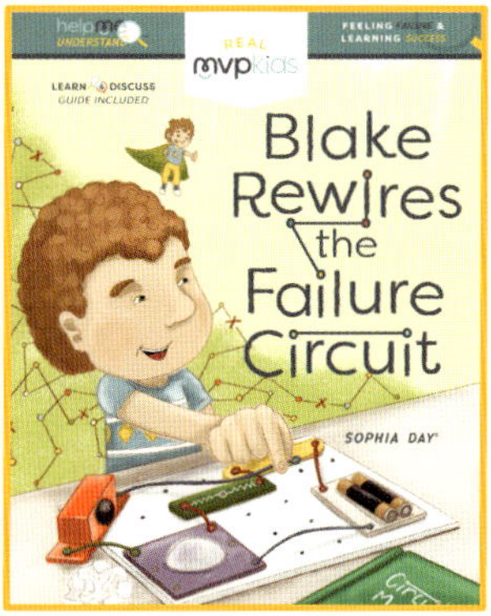

www.mvpkids.com

YONG CHEN
LEO RUSSO
FRANKIE RUSSO
JULIA ROJAS
GABBY GONZÁLEZ
AANYA PATEL
ANNIE JAMES
BLAKE JAMES
SARAH COHEN-GOLDSTEIN